GH01043921

The Sunday

Success with Tomatoes

By Carol Bartlett

Success with Tomatoes is a concise informative guide containing all you need to know to grow tomatoes. It is packed with sound advice, tips and practical suggestions. E book version: 55 pages, 23 illustrations and approximately 12,000 words.

The Sunday gardener is a registered trademark registered 22.02.2012 No 2611342

Carol Bartlett runs the gardening web site and award winning blog, www.sundaygardener.co.uk. Carol created the Sunday Gardener website to share a love of gardening no matter what size your garden or vegetable plot, balcony, terrace or large plot. The idea of the web site is to inspire and encourage others to enjoy gardening and reap the benefits of being outside with nature. Experience the highs and lows, the joys and frustrations of growing all types of plants. No two growing years are ever the same, the garden and seasons are always changing, creating more challenges.

Carol's philosophy is that gardening is a great combination of the therapeutic and practical. It is a cliché, but still true for many, that the garden is a haven, a place in which to relax and escape from the day to day pressures. The title "The Sunday Gardener" is to reflect when, and how, most people fit gardening into their busy week.

TABLE OF CONTENTS

CHAPTER 1 WHAT IS SO GOOD ABOUT GROWING TOMATOES

Tomatoes are a rich and rewarding crop. By following the basic rules you can successfully grow tomatoes and enjoy a bumper crop. Growing tomatoes is not difficult; just time consuming fun. You can grow tomatoes anywhere, in the garden, a greenhouse, in containers, on the patio and if you have no garden, tomatoes will grow on a sunny balcony. This guide will give you all the information you need to grow tomatoes successfully.

From the early stage of nurturing small seedlings and plants, through to supporting the trusses heavy with fruit, growing tomatoes is a challenge with great rewards. There are so many types of tomatoes to choose from and it is easy to produce your own organic supply. Before organic became a buzz word for health, ordinary gardeners were growing tomatoes the organic way. One of the best things about growing tomatoes is the earthy green smell, especially when you handle the plants, or rub the tomatoes leaves; it is the smell of summer gardening.

1. The joys of growing tomatoes

Tomatoes are vigorous plants which grow quickly, and produce abundant crops; by late summer the plants are full of juicy ripe fruit. Home grown tomatoes have a lovely sweet taste, which is all the sweeter when you know you have grown them yourself. To grow sweet juicy tomatoes it is crucial to follow the essential rules of growing tomatoes, in particular to be careful around watering and feeding. In all honestly, tomatoes are not the easiest crop to grow, but by following The Sunday Gardener's tips and advice you will have a successful crop. Tomatoes need regular attention in terms of potting on, watering, feeding, checking the leaf growth and training the plants. Basically they need your time and attention to thrive.

Organic fruit and vegetables sell at a premium and always cost more to buy. One of the clear benefits of growing your own tomatoes, and of growing any veg, is that you are in control of the growing medium for the plants and what sprays and pesticides you use. It is a personal choice which, if any, pest sprays and feeds you use; but it is true to say tomatoes are a crop easily grown without chemicals and using organic feeds. Knowing your tomato crop is clean and clear of pesticides means you can pick and eat the fruit straight from the plant, no need to wash any chemicals away because there are none. You can be confident because you have grown it.

During the summer when the tomatoes are abundant, it is uplifting in any day, especially a working day, to include in your lunch your own home grown tomatoes in salads or sandwiches. In a good growing season you can be picking tomatoes for weeks, especially if you grow varieties which fruit at different times. At some stage all gardeners will get a glut of tomatoes, it's virtually impossible to avoid, but there are plenty of tempting recipes to use up tomatoes. Cooked tomatoes can be made into Pasta sauce which freezes really well for use all the year round. I think that home grown tomatoes make a much more interesting present when visiting friends than the ubiquitous chocolates.

Home grown tomatoes can be good value for money especially in terms of quality, depending in part on how much is spent buying compost, plants, seeds, feeding etc. Growing from seed is the most economical way to grow tomatoes as compared with buying plants. Ordinary seed, as compared to F1 seed (see below) is commonly around £2-3 per packet. If you want to grow different varieties it does mean buying several packets of seeds, but the seeds will keep for several years which reduces the overall cost. Tomatoes are hungry feeders and require a good quality growing medium, usually compost, and regularly feeding with tomato feed all of which have a cost.

Supermarket tomatoes can be quite cheap especially in the summer; the streamlined mass producers of tomatoes grow them very economically. The point is the home grown tomatoes are a different beast. It is yours; you nurtured and grew it, and are now happy to eat it. Supermarkets do have a wide range of tomatoes but it doesn't match the wide range you can grow yourself. Since growing your own veg came of age, and has become popular, even sexy, the garden centres and on line suppliers really push the boat out in relation to ever more varieties to grow.

In addition to old favourites such as Gardener's Delight and Money Maker, there are now hundreds of varieties. You can buy all types and colours from almost black tomatoes, all shades of yellow and orange, tiny bite sized cherries, large ribbed beefsteaks, and even pink tomatoes.

Growing your own tomatoes enables you to experiment and select individual varieties to try out. Tomatoes are still good value for money even if you buy as plants, which can be purchased as small plug plants and grown on.

You can grow tomatoes anywhere and they are the ideal container plant, even on a small balcony. If I could only grow one vegetable it would be tomatoes. For their taste, lovely colour, the great green tomato smell and for the pleasure of nurturing them from seedling to fruit. They may require attention, tomatoes are not instant, but to me and thousands of other gardeners, that is all part of the fun of gardening.

CHAPTER 2 PLANTS V SEEDS

Now we know why we want to grow tomatoes, next is how.

The first decision to make is whether to grow tomatoes from plants or seeds. Several factors will help decide this.

Cost can be factor as clearly plants are more expensive than seed, and the more mature the plant at the time of purchase, the greater the cost. One of the advantages of buying young plants is that it avoids the germination stage and having to grow on little seedlings for which you need a benign environment. Tomato plants are not hardy, which means if you germinate early in the year when it is colder, around March/April, as will usually be the case, you need somewhere warm for the seedlings to carry on growing until they are ready to be planted outside, or it is warm enough to transfer them to an unheated greenhouse or poly tunnel. The same applies if you buy tomato plants at the plug plant size, which are smaller and cheaper as you are buying a more immature plant. The smaller plant will need growing on in warm, frost free area. Plug sized tomato plants are sold earlier in the year when the risk of frost is still present. Do not be fooled into thinking because they are on sale that they are ready for the outside; they are not and need a warmer place to mature.

Larger plants are sold later in the year, but until your garden is completely frost free, they also need to be protected from cold and frost. As to when is the best time to plant tomatoes outside this varies around the country, from south to north in the UK, but the important point is tomato plants will not withstand cold or frost. If you are growing outside the single point to bear in mind is that tomatoes like warmth, and will not tolerate frost. If you have nowhere warm to put seedlings and small plants, (conservatory, porch, window sill, and unused room) it is best to delay buying plants until after the risk of frost has passed. As a rule of thumb, the risk of frost has usually passed everywhere in the U.K. by the end of May/beginning of June.

When and what size of tomato you choose to grow is, in part, a timing issue. The growing season is only so long. To get a crop early in the year, you will need to either germinate from seed early, say February/March. Or alternatively, skip the germination stage and buy larger plants later, around April/May. If you start earlier with a larger plant, you will have tomatoes earlier. Also bear in mind the larger sized tomatoes take longer to mature. It takes time for a plant to grow to maturity and produce tomatoes and if you germinate too late in the year it can be a struggle to get the plant to fruit earlier enough to enjoy the tomatoes before the chill of autumn comes in. This will be less of a problem if you garden in a sheltered, southern part of the UK with good light levels, and more of an issue if you garden in an area prone to low light through rain and cloud cover, and also when the country experiences a bad summer. Tomatoes don't just like warmth, they like good light and sun as well, and the more they get the quicker they grow.

2. Tomato seedlings

If you don't want to germinate from seed, tomato plants can be bought at all stages from small seedlings as in image No 2, to sturdy plants which are showing signs of flower and even of early fruit. It is a personal choice and much depends on how much space you have to keep the plants until ready for outdoor planting. Smaller plants will always be cheaper because you do all the ongoing work, watering, keeping them warm, re potting etc. One suggestion to get a good crop, which I do most years, balancing effort and cost, is to buy a small number of plants and in addition germinate some tomatoes from seed as well, which provides the best of both worlds. If your growing conditions are less than ideal, this is worth considering, especially if you want grow the larger Beefsteak type tomatoes which take longer for the fruit to ripen, (more warmth, light and time.) If you do want to grow beefsteak varieties it maybe more efficient to buy plants. The larger tomatoes take longer to ripen and buying a mature plant will give you a head start as compared with growing from seed or plug plants.

What About F1 seed and Grafted Plants, Are These Better?

In straightforward terms F1 hybrid seed is created by a lengthy process where the grower crosses two pure strains of the plant to produce a variety which has the best qualities of the parent plants. This creates seeds which are designed to be more vigorous and to produce heavier yields. It is an expensive, time consuming process, which is why the seed is always more expensive. In theory F1 seed should produce a better all-round plant, although should you try and save its seed for use the following year, it will not come true and you will not get the same tomato from the saved seed.

Grafted tomato plants are different from F1 hybrid seed. Again, they are more expensive because of the time consuming process of grafting together two plants, a disease resistant rootstock and a tasty variety of tomatoes to combine these qualities. Grafted plants are promoted as being more vigorous, capable of producing higher yields, and resistant to disease. Their unique feature is being strong on disease resistance, because of specially developed disease resistant rootstock. This means they are good to grow in situations where disease maybe a problem, such as outside in the garden or veg plot, where there is a greater risk of Blight (see Chapter 8 Troubleshooting) especially if you are using the same growing area on a regular basis.

3. Young grafted tomato plant

It is also widely stated that grafted plants fruit earlier and yield more. I have found grafted plants to be very good, but they are two or three times more expensive than standard plants. Again a good compromise would be to buy a grafted plant only of the larger Beefsteak varieties, or as a tomato plant to grow outside, which would give the plant extra growing vigour and disease resistance.

Key tips

1. With grafted plants it is very important not too plant deeply. You can see the graft above the soil level on the plant; it is a visible join. In image 3 above, the graft lies within the protective sleeve. Always

plant grafted plants with the graft above soil level. This is because if you plant so that the graft join is below soil level, it will cause the plant to throw out extra roots above the graft, which could then pick up diseases to which the plant is not resistant making it pointless buying a grafted plant.

2. Avoid germinating from seed too late, if it gets to May and you haven't germinated it is better to buy plants at this stage because there will not be enough time for the germinated plants to get to maturity to harvest a decent crop.

3. Keep an eye on the weather, take care to keep seedlings and plants frost free and warm.

CHAPTER 3 DIFFERENT TYPES OF TOMATOES

There are two basic types of tomato plants in terms of growing requirements. They are (1) Bush (2) Cordon, and the main different between them is their growth habit. The Cordon tomato has upright growth trained to have one single stem and grows tall. Bush as the name suggests, is bushier, much shorter and has several stems. Cordon tomatoes are also known as Indeterminate and are always grown as a single stem. They are very vigorous and will easily reach up to 1.5- 1.8 metres in height. Bush or Determinate are smaller, bushier with flowers and fruits at the end of the branches. Many of the varieties suitable for small containers and hanging baskets, such as Tumbling tom, are bush varieties.

Cordon tomato growing requirements are more complicated than those of Bush tomatoes but with good rewards. Within these two divisions are all the different varieties of tomatoes such as cherry, salad, plum, beefsteak and many variations in between. When deciding which variety of tomato to grow bear in mind the larger the tomato the more heat, light and growing time it requires. This means cherry tomatoes will generally fruit ahead of a Beefsteak and if you garden in an exposed area with poor light levels growing Beefsteak tomatoes will be more challenging. There is a big difference in growing conditions across the UK, which means growing Beefsteak tomatoes on the south coast of England will be easier than in Northern England which can often be wetter and cooler. All Gardening books and advice are a guide and have to be adjusted according to where you garden, the micro climate of your garden, and the prevailing summer conditions in any given year. When considering which types of tomatoes to grow bear in mind the ideal growing conditions for all tomatoes is sheltered and sunny.

Whilst there are two basic types of tomatoes, there is now a huge array of varieties to grow which can be a bit baffling. There are literally dozens of varieties offered for sale in garden centres and on line. Which to choose is, as always, a personal choice. A good starting point is to buy a small selection of different plants or seeds so that you can compare. Helpfully, some companies now display customer ratings which give additional information. The sweetness of the tomatoes is determined by the variety and how it is grown. Good light levels with regular watering and feeding can make all the difference and a sweeter tomato.

Recommended Varieties of Tomatoes To Grow

Although this section is called recommended varieties to grow, there are now such a variety of tomatoes on the market it is hard to make recommendations. Many existing tomato varieties are very good, and with each growing season the retailers bring out yet more new varieties. I have had great success with all sorts of tomatoes from cherry to beefsteak, and much depends on personal preference and what you want to do with your tomatoes. For example, if you want to make pasta sauces, cherry tomatoes are not going to work well because of their size, there is little flesh to make the sauce, but they are very suitable for salads.

Below are a selection of very well-known, tried and tested tomatoes which are widely available. It is a good idea to hedge your bets and grow several varieties and it is also more interesting. Another advantage of growing a selection of different types of tomato is that when planning your crop, in early spring, we have no idea what sort of summer will arrive and by growing different types of tomatoes you have a better chance of success whatever the weather.

Any varieties which have the RHS AGM (Royal Horticultural Society Award of Garden Merit), are always a good bet. These vegetables have been put through trials by the RHS for their garden qualities and disease resistance. Varieties listed below are reliable to grow with good flavour and germinate easily from seed.

'Sungold' sweet and orange skinned suitable for greenhouse and outdoor growing. 'Alicante' AGM is a medium sized red skinned tomato.

'Gardener's Delight' AGM A cherry type with red fruits with grows in a greenhouse or outdoors. 'Shirley' AGM this is an early tomato suitable for a greenhouse.

'Golden Sunrise' is another yellow skinned, medium sized tomato which can be grown in the greenhouse or outdoors.

Good bush varieties for hanging baskets and smaller containers are the Tumbling toms red and yellow; a suitable outdoor bush variety is 'Tornado'

For Beefsteak type 'Brandywine' is much recommended and 'Roma' is a widely grown plum type.

Said to be Blight resistant, 'Crimson Crush'F1, 'Mountain Magic'F1 and 'Lizzano'F1 worth checking out particularly if you intend to grow tomatoes outside. Outdoor grown tomatoes are more prone to Blight which is very difficult to eradicate (see troubleshooting Chapter 7.)

4. Different sizes and varieties of tomatoes

Key tips

1. Select varieties of tomatoes suitable for your growing conditions.
2. Consider growing more disease resistant tomatoes outside including grafted plants, and the larger tomatoes in the most sheltered spots with plenty of light and warmth.

CHAPTER 4 WHERE TO GROW TOMATOES

There is lots of choice around where to grow tomatoes. It is true to say, in the right conditions tomatoes can be grown outside, under glass, in containers, grow bags and hanging baskets, almost anywhere. Whether inside or out, tomatoes need light, ideally at least 6 hours sunlight and better still 8 hours per day. They need shelter, warmth and sunshine. The plant converts light into energy and that energy drives the plant to grow, and produce flowers and fruit. Equally tomatoes do not like it too hot which can cause the plant to dry out, which is one of the main causes of split skins on the fruit at harvest time, and impaired flavour.

Growing Tomatoes Outside

Wherever you grow tomatoes, particularly if growing outside, the fundamental starting point is that tomatoes require a sheltered spot away from wind, with plenty of warmth, sun, light and good organically enriched soil. Before planting outside dig in organic matter and some fertiliser. This is important because tomatoes are hungry plants. The soil should be friable, that is to say not compacted, free draining, and contain plenty of organic material. Ideally, if you are intending to grow tomatoes outside in the vegetable plot, it is a good idea either in the autumn or over the winter, to dig in some well-rotted manure. If time has run out on this option, dig in some good compost in the spring before planting. Raised veg beds are good as they enable you, over time, to add more and more organic material to the soil enriching the beds, and it is easier to keep weed free. If you do pick up manure from a local stables it is essential that it is well rotted, otherwise it can spread weed seed which is not what you want in the veg plot. Whether in the garden, veg plot or raised beds the soil needs to be broken up so that is a fine tilth, meaning no lumps or stones.

5. Tomatoes planted outside

An advantage of growing tomatoes outside is that it is often easier to water the plants. The ground outside is less prone, as compared to containers, to being overwatered or drying out, making watering easier and more effective. Being in the ground as compared to containers, there are less extremes of temperature and moisture.   Tomatoes have an optimum temperature range for good growth of between 21- 24 C. In a greenhouse on a sunny day it can be very hot and exceed this range. The downside to growing tomatoes outside is that if we experience a cool and wet summer with temperatures often below 21C, not uncommon in northern England, there will be less fruit to be harvested. Unless your garden is sheltered and in a warm spot, you may be more successful growing tomatoes in a greenhouse. A conservatory may sound like a good idea, and it may be good for the initial germination and growing on of young plants, but a conservatory will be too hot in the summer for mature plants.

If you are growing tomatoes outside it is best to select varieties which are bred for outside growth and to plant with around 45 cms between plants to give growing space. 'Gardeners delight' and 'Money Maker' are good outside tomatoes. Also, because tomato Blight is more of a problem for outdoor grown tomatoes than greenhouse types, it is a good idea to select a variety which is Blight resistant. In addition, to reduce the chances of Blight it is important if you grow tomatoes outside to rotate your crop each year.

Crop rotation is the system whereby you rotate, or change where you plant your veg each year so that you do not put the same type of veg in the same bit of the veg plot each year, but rotate the type of vegetables around the plot or garden. For the purpose of crop rotation vegetables are divided into four groups, namely Legumes, Alliums, Roots and Brassicas. Tomatoes are classified as roots, so you would not plant tomatoes in the same part of the veg plot where you have previously planted roots, for example Tomatoes or Potatoes. The same applies to Alliums, the idea is that you do not plant Garlic where you planted say Leeks the previous year. You move the crops around the veg plot so where in year 1 you planted legumes such as beans and peas, the next year you would plant roots say tomatoes and/or potatoes and the next year Alliums, such as leeks or garlic. To keep track of this, I have a note or photograph of what was planted where in the veg plot and I make sure I change the planting around for the next year. This helps to avoid build-up of disease in the soil and keeps the plants healthier.

Growing Tomatoes in a Greenhouse or Poly tunnel

Growing tomatoes in a greenhouse or poly tunnel has distinct advantages because it creates a protected environment, especially early in the year and during poor spells, when the weather can be cool and windy none of which suits tomato plants. A greenhouse is an ideal spot for bringing on seedlings and young plants and the protected environment is good for growing tomatoes. In some areas of the country a greenhouse is a great advantage when growing tomatoes. I garden in an exposed area, which is also a frost pocket, as a result growing tomatoes outside is unpredictable. I have succeeded many times growing tomatoes outside, but only when the tomatoes have been started in the greenhouse and grown on to a good size, and then planted out in containers, on a south facing patio in a good summer and the key is a good summer.

The problem is when you start out at the beginning of the year, seeding and planning, there is no way of knowing what sort of summer is going to come along. It is very disheartening to do everything right but be thwarted by a poor, cool wet summer. I always hedge my bets by growing some tomatoes outside and some in the greenhouse as well. As a result of a succession of average to poor summers I grow more tomatoes in the greenhouse. If you are thinking of growing tomatoes outside in a warmer, more sheltered part of the UK you can be very successful providing they are planted in the right spot, (sheltered and sunny) and in well prepared ground. If conditions are not ideal and you do not have a greenhouse or small poly tunnel, the important point will be to place the tomatoes in the warmest, most sheltered spot in your garden.

Poly tunnels are a cheaper alternative to a greenhouse and excellent for growing all sorts of fruit and veg. There can be a problem with Botrytis, (Grey mould) when growing tomatoes in a poly tunnel or greenhouse. Botrytis is caused by a fungal infection which in the summer thrives in humid conditions, and in the winter in cold and damp still air. To keep at bay ventilation is very important; a good airflow is essential to reduce the risk of Botrytis. For both the greenhouse and poly tunnel ventilation is also very important in high summer to reduce the temperature, and prevent the tomatoes from overheating.

6. A neat example from an RHS garden of Cordon tomatoes growing in a greenhouse; note the single upright stem and cane support.

Container Grown Tomatoes

Tomatoes are very suitable to grow in containers of all sorts. Condon varieties, because they grow so tall, will need a large container, in which there is room to place at least one stake for stem support and extra supports for the heavy branches when they have tomato fruits on them. When growing Cordon tomatoes outside in containers, I always put a few crocks or stones in the base of the container to add weight to reduce the chances of the wind blowing the plant over. Ideally you will place the container out of the wind, but our summers are unpredictable. Placing crocks in the bottom of a container is also said to aid drainage.

Tomatoes need a good sized pot or container to have enough compost and room for the roots. The minimum size for one plant is 20 cms (10") to 30 cms (12"). Use as large a pot as you can because the larger the pot, the more compost and water it will hold, which will reduce the risk of the plant drying out. Apart from the damage drying out can cause, (which could kill the plant,) drying out by definition will subject the plant to irregular watering which can impair flavour and cause the skins to split and also encourage blossom end rot, (see troubleshooting Chapter 7.)

Cordon tomatoes are tall and upright plants with one single stem which needs tying in to a long cane or stake, see image 6. Later in the season the branches with fruit can be so heavy as to snap and may need extra support, see image 13. There are many commercially produced tomato supports all of which come at a price. It is easy to make your own supports using canes and sticks, see image 14 free stakes below, and I always keep pruning off cuts from all sorts of shrubs to make supports.

Tomatoes are widely grown in containers, large plant pots, grow bags and more recently hanging baskets. It may be easier in smaller containers and hanging baskets to grow bush varieties, and those tomato varieties especially developed for hanging baskets such as 'Tumbling Tom', 'Cherry Cascade' and 'Romello'. The smaller the container, the more prone it is to drying out, which means the routine of regular watering is very important. It follows that hanging baskets, which tend to be the smallest of containers, are the most susceptible to drying out and will need to be watered every day during warm weather.

A possible way to avoid drying out is to add into the compost water retaining gel, which is specially sold for this purpose by the garden retailers. It will reduce the risk of the basket drying out but there are some points to be aware of. You need to follow the instructions on the packet very carefully as the gel really does swell up a lot. If too much gel mixture is added to the compost it can swell up too much, which will push the tomato plant upwards, and disturb its roots. Secondly, the gel is made up of chemicals and you may not want to add this to the growing medium, it's a personal choice.

If space is limited in your garden or vegetable plot, or you have no garden and are relying on a balcony or patio, tomatoes are one of the vegetables most suitable for patio and container growing. In practical terms it may be easier to grow bush varieties, but as long as they are kept well-watered with plenty of sun all sorts of tomatoes will be happy on growing on a balcony.

7. Tomatoes growing on a balcony and in a grow bag

Using Grow Bags

Grow bags have become popular for growing all types of vegetables including tomatoes. The compost mix in the grow bag is sold as ideally suited for tomatoes to facilitate a good crop, but at a price. I find that one of the problems when growing tomatoes in grow bags, as compared to containers, (as shown in image 8,) is the lack of depth; the compost is quite shallow. Grow bags are not as deep as a good sized trough or container. To reduce this problem and increase the depth of the grow bag, use tape such as masking tape to reshape the grow bag, or supports to hold the bag together and give it more of a rounded shape. The grow bag in image 7 above has been re shaped (in this case by using supports) to make it deeper and more dome shaped, when compared with the grow bag in image 8 below, which is very flat. Whether flat or taped up to be more rounded, another problem with grow bags is when watering there is a tendency for the water to run off and not soak in.

In the image 8 plastic rings have been added which sit on the top of the grow bag. This creates a better growing environment because it increase the soil depth, helps to direct water to the plant and prevent run off. You can avoid the expense of buying rings by cutting out the base of large pots and sinking them into a grow bag. You can then top up the soil level within the pot and use it to direct the water.

Some growers advocate using two grow bags, one on top of the other, and using a plant pot with the bottom cut out or a ring to sink into the grow bag and plant into. This will help but it is more expensive. Another alternative is to empty the contents of the grow bags into containers to use the quality compost. However, doing this does raise the question as to the merits of buying grow bags in the first place?

Although a little obscured by the tomato foliage, in the image 7 above, there are actually two plastic water bottles sunk into the grow bag between the plants to aid watering. Before placing the bottles in the grow bag, cut the bottom off, so it forms a funnel directing more water to the roots. Using water bottles in this way works well in lots of situations where you want to be sure to get water to the roots. For example, when planting on a sloping bank where the water may naturally run off, or around a new plant to make sure it gets enough water to the roots to get off to a good start. Given that irregular watering affects the flavour of the tomato and can cause the skin to split, if you are using grow bags it is important to ensure the water goes to the plants roots and doesn't run off. With grow bags, it is more difficult to water well, and if the bag does dry out, it is hard to rehydrate.

If you are using grow bags, I would recommend giving the bags a really good shake before you plant up. Grow bags are often stacked up on top of each other at garden centres and the compost can be compacted and lumpy. Giving it a good shake will help to break it up and make sure the compost is free flowing so the roots can grow easily, without obstruction.

There are some advantages to using grow bags. They are convenient, the compost is ideally blended for tomatoes and there is no need to buy pots or containers as you can plant straight in. However, it is important to purchase peat free grow bags to preserve the natural growing environment of peat. This is particularly so because Peatlands are the largest natural terrestrial carbon store and of huge ecological importance.

8. Flat grow bag and use of Rings without which the soil depth would be very shallow.

Key tips.

1. Tomatoes are ideal for growing in all types of containers, but as container grown plants they are more prone to drying out. Grow in the largest container you have. Grow bags maybe convenient, but be aware of their limitations.

2. If you have problems with Blight consider growing tomatoes in a greenhouse or poly tunnel.

3. Grow bags are convenient but maybe on the shallow side, considered adding rings to increase the depth and ease of watering.

CHAPTER 5 HOW TO GROW TOMATOES DETAILED TIPS AND ADVICE

Stage 1 Growing From Seed

Germinating and growing tomatoes from seed is cheap and relatively easy. The good news is that most packets of tomato seed, (although not F1 hybrids,) contain a lot of seed so if at first you do not succeed, seed again. Seedlings are delicate and need a controlled environment, and careful handling. You can buy special seed compost, such as from the John Innes range. Seed compost is a careful blend designed to aid germination. The downside is that it is more expensive to buy different composts for different plants.

I find tomato seed germinates just fine using ordinary peat free compost. If the compost is a bit chunky, which can often be the case especially with peat free composts, sieve it so that the compost is fine. Tomato seed will keep from one year to the next so you can re-use any unused seed in future years. To store seed for the next year keep in a cool dry place. At the end of the season I put unused seeds in a tin and store it in the fridge or cool garage. Metal containers are best because any form of plastic container is likely to produce condensation and moisture, will cause the seed to become damp and possibly rot, as a result it will no longer be viable.

9. Tomato seeds are very small

If you are intending to grow your tomatoes outside you will need to germinate the seed about 8 weeks before the likely time of the last frost. In most parts of the UK this means germinating in March/April, more April than March in the colder regions of the UK. Tomatoes destined for a greenhouse can be sown earlier. You will see from image 9 above that tomato seeds are small. The seeds illustrated are not new seed, but last year's seed which has been stored in a refrigerator over the winter. I always sow last year's seed first, and only if it fails to germinate do I go to the expense of buying new seed. As each packet contains many seeds this is a more economical way to grow tomatoes.

Place two or three seeds into a small 3" /7cm pot and sprinkle lightly with compost, mist a little with a fine water spray so the compost is just damp, taking care not to over water or the seed will rot and not germinate. To germinate, seeds need some warmth, between 18 – 22 C degrees. If you are germinating later in the year, mid-April or May there will be enough warmth on sunny days if you place the pot in a greenhouse.

Earlier in the year when temperatures are still cool, extra help is needed. I use a propagator and/ or a heated mat, or place the pot on a sunny window sill to raise the temperature for germination. The propagator tray/plant pot can sit on top of the heat source to create the extra warmth for germination or you can use the propagator on its own. I also find it helps, prior to seeding, to move the bag of compost inside into the greenhouse or conservatory to warm it up a little, especially if you are germinating early in the year. Compost stored outside can be very cold and wet.

A propagator helps to regulate the growing environment in terms of warmth and moisture; you can usually see water droplets forming on the inside of the propagator. If you don't have a propagator it is easy and cheap to make a simple one by putting a plastic bag over the top of the pot and securing it with an elastic band so it is similar to a sealed unit. To keep the bag from resting on the seeding when it emerges, insert a small stick as a prop to hold the bag upright. In image 10 below a home-made propagator is placed on the windowsill in a conservatory and I would expect germination in about a week to 10 days. Once small seedlings are established remove the bag.

10. Home-made propagator suitable for tomato seed germination

The essentials for tomato seeds to germinate and grow are water, air and warmth. Germination requires that the container does not dry out and whilst you can keep an eye on it and mist occasionally, it is often easier to place the small pot in a propagator. This ensures an even temperature, and because the unit is sealed, moisture is retained creating an ideal atmosphere for germination. It is important not to keep the seedling in the propagator for too long. This is because the warm fug within the propagator is good for germination, but if the seedlings are growing in it for too long, it can make the seedling soft and sappy. For this reason it is best to remove the seedling from the propagator once they are established. This may sound contradictory, on the one hand it is important to take seedlings out of the propagator once established, and on the other hand, the seedlings need to grow on in warm, frost free conditions. For this reason if temperatures drop in a cold spell, or overnight, you may need to put the seedlings back in the propagator as a temporary measure.

Tomato plants are not hardy and need to be protected from cold and they cannot be placed outside until late spring. To keep at the right temperature put seedlings on a window sill, conservatory, and greenhouse or under glass until late May when the risk of frost has passed. Best temperatures for seedlings is around 65F degrees, (17C) and it is not good to let the temperature drop much below 45F degrees (7 C); temperatures below 35F degrees (2C) can kill the seedlings. If you are growing on seedlings in a greenhouse, which will provide good light and growing conditions, you just need to check if nights are cool, or there is an occasional frost, protect the small plants using a propagator or plastic cover.

For seedlings to grow well, they want good light preferably coming from all directions, ideally 360 degrees. This is possible in a greenhouse, but often an unheated greenhouse is not warm enough until later in the year. For this reason you often need to start germinating and growing young seedlings indoors. Conservatories are good, and tomatoes seedlings can also be grown in porches and on windowsills. Light levels are important. When there is light from one side, such as happens on a window sill, it causes the seedlings to stretch towards the light. When this happens, seedling become leggy, which is weak and spindly. To manage the problem of low light and one sided light sources, the pot needs to be turned regularly to create even growth, and if you are growing seedlings in the house, turn the pot each day.

The ideal seedling is upright with a strong stem; with less than ideal conditions the seedling may look as in image 11 below, not a strong stem and leggy. All is not lost, if the seedling is otherwise healthy, the solution is to repot the seedling sinking the stem deeper into the compost than it was previously planted so that the weedy part of the seedling is below the soil and 9 times out of 10 it will grow on fine. The second image shows the re potted seedling. I have salvaged seedlings this way which have gone on to become fine tomato plants.

11. Weedy seedling (top image) improved by re-potting (bottom image)

Key tips

1. For best results place seedlings in a propagator and grow on in warm conditions.
2. Turn the pot regularly to ensure even growth and to stop the seedling becoming leggy.
3. Repot leggy seedlings deeper into the compost burying the leggy part.
4. Keep seeds from year to year storing over winter in a cool place.

Stage 2 Potting On

A simple but important step. Tomatoes grow best in the right sized pot. When tomatoes have grown and become too large for their current pot, tomatoes need to be potted on into the next size pot, and then finally into the largest container in which they will grow all summer. It's a bit time consuming, but if you pot up a small seedling into a large a pot, it will not thrive. When you are re-potting, handle the seedling very carefully by the leaves, taking care not to touch the stem, and pot into the next sized pot. If you are growing from seed, the seedling will need to be potted on for the first time in about a month, by which time it should have filled out the small pot out with tiny roots, see image12 (top right) below.

If you are raising a plant purchased from the garden centre, pot it on when it looks too big for the pot as shown in images 12 (top left) below. In this image, the tomato plants in pots standing on the potting bench look too big for the pots they are in, they look top heavy, a sure sign they are ready for potting on. Once the plant has outgrown its pot size, move up a pot size and finally into the largest container for the rest of the summer. Each time you pot on, plant the stem a little lower into the compost as this will aid root growth, unless it is a grafted plant, when it is essential to repot at the same soil level.

When potting on it is important to press down gently on the soil to make sure the plant is firmly anchored in and there are no air pockets. If the tomato plant's roots grow into an air pocket, where there is no soil or nutrient, the root will not grow well which is why it is important to press down to make sure all air pockets are removed. When re potting Cordon types you will need to put a small support in the container, with a loose tie to provide support, see images 12 (bottom right) below.

The final container for a tomato plant needs to be a good size, the larger the better. Small containers are more prone to drying out and there is less room for the roots. They are also less stable which means they are more prone to being blown over. Ideally, the final container should be between 30-40cms and the top of the size range is best.

12. Potting on procedure

Tomato plants are sensitive to cold and if you are going to plant outside, you will need to "harden off" the plants first before planting out permanently. It would be too much of a shock to take a plant from a controlled environment in the greenhouse or under glass, and put it outside exposed to all elements and where it is colder. If it is too cold and frosty, it will kill a tomato plant because they are not frost hardy. Don't be fooled just because it is not frosty that is OK to put or plant the tomato outside. Low temperatures and the change in temperature from mild conditions indoors to less clement outside conditions can arrest the plant's growth and it may take some weeks to recover. Low temperatures will also cause leaf curl.

"Hardening off" means to prepare the plant gradually for the outside conditions. To do this plants should be placed outside on mild days to acclimatise, gradually increasing the length of time so the plant is outside for increasingly longer periods, until the plant is outside all of the time. Even so beware of cold nights which are frost free but chilly.

Either bring the plant back into the greenhouse if a particularly cold night is forecast or wrap it in a fleece. When the plant is fully hardened off it can be planted or left permanently outside. This works for all young plants and for bedding plants which, like tomato plants, are sold early in the year from March onwards but are not ready for outside planting.

If you buy a young tomato plant in March, you will need to pot it on and harden it off before it is ready to grow outside. Ideal growing temperature for tomatoes are between 21-25C degrees (70-75F) and tomatoes are not happy below 16C degrees (61F) or above 27C (81F). If you get caught out, and a cold night is forecast even if there is no frost, move the plant under cover, or cover with a fleece or cloche overnight.

Key tips

1. Plant tomatoes in pots proportionate to their size, and keep frost free.
2. Harden off before planting outside.

Stage 3 Staking and Supporting Tomatoes

Wherever you intend to grow tomatoes, outside or in the greenhouse, if you are growing the tall variety (Cordon) you must stake them. They need good sturdy supports using canes, wood stakes, or you can use commercially produced tomatoes supports. The cheapest, and often the easiest to use, are canes or wood stakes as in image 14 below. It is best to insert a support each time you pot on the tomato using the largest support when planting into its final container, grow bag or growing space. When potting up into the final container, the support needs to be much larger than the plant, up to 1.8 metres for a Cordon tomato to take into account further upwards growth.

You will need to place the support close to the plant so that you can easily tie in the plant. I like to use off cuts from pruning as the irregular shape of the supports gives plenty of scope for supporting the weighty branches of tomatoes later in the year when the fruit has formed.

Image 13 shows what can happen if the plant is not properly supported. The weight of the fruit can cause the branches to bend over, and even to snap. The tomato fruits are quite heavy, which means as the plant matures, it is important to keep an eye on the branches and fruit. It may be necessary to add extra ties, and to directly support the fruit to ensure the branches do not bend and get damaged.

13. Heavy tomato fruits causing stem to break

As illustrated it is not just Cordon tomatoes which are prone to the branches bending and snapping, this can happen even with bush tomatoes. In addition if you are growing Bush tomatoes outside a support will help to keep the fruit clean and off the ground, as in the image 15 below. There are a whole raft of supports which can be purchased as suitable for tomatoes. For example, the grow bag frame in illustration 7 above, plant rings, halos, individual plant cages, wood frames, and many more. If you Google "tomato plant support images" there are dozens of different types of supports, some home-made, others commercial.

It is a matter of choice; personally if you are growing just a few plants, canes and pruning off cuts will do the job well for free. In image 14 below, it may look at first glance like just a bunch of sticks, but looking at them more closely, it is clear that they would make good supports for all sorts of plants including tomatoes. These are off cuts from pruning, in this case an Elaeagnus. I think they look nicer, more natural in the garden and veg plot as plant supports compared with metal supports. When selecting your tomato plant support, bear in mind the eventual height of the Cordon plant may well be 1.5 -1.8m (6ft)

14 Free natural plant supports

15. Bush tomato under planted with Rosemary supported by a metal frame

Key tips

1. All plants need appropriate supports, and later in the season when there are lots of tomatoes extra support may be needed.
2. Keep any off cuts from pruning to make free supports for tomatoes (and many other garden plants.)

Stage 4 Leaves and Stems

Tomatoes are vigorous and grow like a horticultural train. There is no problem getting a tomato plant to grow. The challenge is to produce tasty fruit and not masses of branches and leaves. Tomato plants will naturally produce lots of leaves but gardeners want fruit. The image below demonstrates the vigour of a tomato plant. This is a tomato plant growing out of crack of soil in a city centre payment. A seed casually discarded, probably from a sandwich, has lodged itself in a crack in the pavement. Sometime later it has germinated, and was growing well when I spotted it and took this image, on my hands and knees on the pavement, much to the amusement of passers-by, but it illustrates the point. Tomatoes are vigorous and grow anywhere, but in poor conditions such as these the plant will produce lots of leaves and growth, but meagre, if any, flowers or fruit.

16. Tomato plant sprouting out from the pavement

Cordon tomatoes should be grown to have one main single stem and several branches, (see image 6.) However, the tomato plant will try to produce lots of side shoots which will create yet more branches and foliage. If left unchecked the plant's energy will go into making more and more side shoots, branches and leaves, at the expense of flowers and fruit. An important part of growing tomatoes is to remove all side shoots every week. This is because those side shoots will form extra, unnecessary branches with little fruit and more foliage. The requirement to remove side shoots can cause confusion to identify which are the branches needed for fruit and flowers, and which are the superfluous side shoots. The image 17 below illustrates the different parts of the tomato plant. The aim is to have one central stem, with various branches, but all side shoots (which always emerge at a right angle between stem and branch,) removed.

17. Removing side shoots: illustration showing side shoots at right angle to the branch and stem.

From an early stage once the plant starts to mature, Cordon tomatoes need to be tied in regularly to the central cane to keep them supported. Below image 18 is an example of how not to tie in a plant. As the plant has grown the tie has cut into the plant stem and damaged it which could lead to disease. Two lessons: firstly ensure ties are looser and more of a loop so there is room for the plant to grow. Secondly, I like to use soft ties and find raffia is very good. It is strong, soft, a natural product which looks nice as a plant tie and is compostable.

It is important when tying in the plant to take care not to accidently constrict sections of the plant, causing them to be pressed together. When the plant is large and with lots of leaves and branches, it is easy when tying in to cause the branches to rub together which can also scrunch up leaves. These are hot spots for disease later in the season as the plant matures. Botrytis, caused by air born spores, will often start where leaves are bunched together or a plant is damaged.

Do not remove side shoots from the bush variety of tomato as its natural shape is to grow many branches, and it is on those branches the flowers and fruit will form. Here the difference between Cordon and Bush tomatoes is important because if you pinch out shoots on the Bush variety, as is routinely done on Cordon tomatoes, it would result in removing flowers and so the fruits, potential reducing the crop.

18. How not to tie in a tomato plant and Raffia makes ideal ties

Key tips

1. Remove all side shoots on a regular basis during the growing season.
2. Take care when tying in plants to ensure ties are not too tight.
3. Do not remove side shoots from Bush varieties.

Stage 5 Watering and Feeding– The Most Important Bit.

Regular watering and feeding is key to getting a good crop of sweet, tasty tomatoes. Tomatoes are hungry feeders and need regular watering and feeding. The aim is to water the compost until moist, but not drenched and do not leave the plant standing in water. Watering needs to be increased as growing progresses, and the plant will naturally take up more water. Always water the soil not the leaves or stem. Watering the leaves, as opposed to the roots, will encourage Blight and other diseases. Image 19 below shows how not to water a tomato plant. The watering can rose should be right down level with the pot, so the water flows onto the soil and roots, and avoids the leaves.

19. How not to water a tomato plant

On hot days on a sunny patio or in the greenhouse, tomato plants should be checked daily to ensure they have not dried out. In warm conditions plants will often need watering daily, even more. If the weather is warm, and it is hot in a greenhouse I also water the floor, as the evaporating water will help to cool the air and reduce the temperature. It does increase the humidity, which can create conditions suitable for Blight and Botrytis, but provided there is plenty of ventilation in the greenhouse I have never found it to be problem. The water evaporates quickly in the strong summer heat.

Botrytis is more of a problem in greenhouses over winter when the air is still and damp. Tomato plants, like people, get stressed if they are very hot. Regular and sufficient watering is the most important tip when growing tomatoes, it is crucial. The soil and the roots should not be allowed to dry out. Poor watering will affect the flavour and later on can lead to skin splitting in ripe fruit and blossom end rot, (see Chapter 7 Troubleshooting)

The tomato plant's need for regular watering means if you are going on holiday you will need to make arrangements to ensure the plants are looked after. A gardening friend or relative to look after the plants is ideal. On a hot summer's day plants will barely last a day on their own and let alone a week. There are some self-watering irrigations systems which if properly set up will water plants for a week, and some more sophisticated systems which will provide water for longer. I prefer a gardening friend to be sure all is going well.

In addition to watering, the other essential for tomatoes to produce good quality tasty fruit, is regular feeding. The required tomato food is a high potash feed. All plant foods have Nitrogen (N) Phosphorus (P) and Potassium or Potash (K) which is marked on the pack as these letters. It is easy to buy good Tomato food there are plenty on the market. Looking at the information on the bottle, tomato food should have proportions where the K element is higher than the other elements. Just a note in passing, tomato food is only suitable for certain other veg, such as courgettes, and not universally suitable for all vegetables. It is not interchangeable with a general plant food.

Start feeding tomato plants when the first truss (flowers) have appeared and carry on feeding initially weekly and then twice weekly as the plant matures and starts to produce more flowers and fruit. Keep the feeding regime in accordance with the directions on the bottle. The strength of tomato varies and it is possible to overfeed plants, so be sure to dilute according to instructions.

I also recommend removing some of the tomato leaves, sometimes called "de leafing." The early leaves at the base of the plant often turn yellow and these are best removed. I also remove a few leaves each week once the plant is mature to aid air flow and which helps to concentrate the nutrients flowing to the leaves and fruit which are left. As previously stated, tomatoes are vigorous and removing some leaves will not damage the plant. Some growers, and certainly commercial growers, often recommend removing many more of the leaves, almost denuding the plant. I do not do this, but I do remove a good amount of leaves especially later on in the season when the plants are more prone to pests and diseases. You want to increase air flow to reduce the risk of disease.

20. Tomato flowers

To get a good crop of tomatoes a plant also needs to have plenty of fertilised flowers which have time to mature into fruits. Tomato flowers are shown in image 20 and have both male, (anthers) and female parts (stigma) which means they self-pollinate. A breeze needs to blow the pollen from the male part to the female part. If tomatoes are grown outside this will occur naturally with our weather conditions. In a greenhouse Bumblebees will be attracted to the tomato flowers and are great pollinators, leave the door, windows and vents open to let the bees in, (and out) and this will suffice to produce pollination.

In Iceland, they grow tomatoes in glasshouses where on the face of it, conditions are not ideal. The Icelandic people have cleverly harnessed the heat and power from the thermal springs to warm their glasshouses in which to grow tomato plants, and other salad crops. However, to get pollination they have to import bees and set them free in the glasshouses. It is interesting to see the Icelandic growers literally have a box full of bees which they let loose in the glasshouse.

Given that tomato plants are so vigorous and they will keep growing upwards at some point they need to be stopped. Each layer of flowers is called a truss and there is gardening debate about how many layers or trusses should be left on the plant. It depends a bit on the summer as in a good summer more fruit will ripen so you can leave more trusses in place. A rule of thumb is 4- 5 trusses on indoor plants and 3-4 on outdoor plants. Also 4-5 layers of flowers will very likely take the tomato plant to up around 1.5/1.8 metres or 6ft, about the height of many greenhouses.

Once the plant is this tall stop it growing any further by taking out the growing point. This means you cut off the top of the plant. Cutting this off may include some flowers and growth, but once the tomato plant has reached this stage of maturity you need to stop it growing any taller. You will find once you have cut off the top of the plant, within a short time a week or so, the tomato plant will re grow. It will keep growing producing more growth, and you will need to keep checking it and cutting back until the end of the season.

Next, as the season moves on it's a question of taking stock. Not all the flowers or small fruits on the tomato plant will have time, in terms of light, heat and remaining time left in the growing season for the fruit to ripen. You want the plant to put its energy into ripening the more mature tomatoes. Later in the growing season around September, (depending on your local conditions, and whether it is a good or bad summer,) you need to take a hard look and be a bit ruthless. You need to decide which fruit to keep and which are not going to mature in time. At this late stage in the summer, tiny fruits and flowers are unlikely to form decent sized tomatoes before the season comes to an end. I remove all immature fruits and flowers to help ripen the remaining tomatoes. There comes a point when it is clear that the small fruits and flowers are not going to amount to anything. Time to cut your losses, literally, and remove them.

Key tips

1. Regular watering and feeding is the essential and most important tip.
2. Stop the plants growing at between 3-5 trusses.
3. Open vents and doors to let the bees in and out.
4. Later in the season take stock and be bold, cut off any flowers and fruits which are too immature.

CHAPTER 6 HARVEST

The best time. Picking lovely warm fruits ready to eat or pack into a lunch box. No more shopping for tomatoes, just step outside. It is hard not to feel a bit smug when you look at the fruits of your labour. It definitely gives you a buzz. But, what to do with all the green tomatoes?

Get them to ripen. The Sunday Gardener has, I would say a fool proof method to ripen tomatoes but to call it that may invite challenge. Instead I will say The Sunday Gardener has a good way of ripening tomatoes. Many years ago I misjudged a house move and had to move in late in the summer, when several tomato plants in the greenhouse were covered in green fruit. Originally, I mistakenly conceived various ways to transport the plants with our furniture, but soon realised this was not practical. Instead I cut the fruit on vines and in the new house laid them out on newspaper in the conservatory, where it was warm and sunny. About 80% ripened nicely. I recommend at the end of the growing season usually around late October or November, depending on the weather, that you cut any unripe fruit from the plants on the vine and bring it inside to a conservatory or warm window sill and watch it ripen. Many growers advocate the opposite, to put the fruit in a dark box or draw. My experience has been that it is better to place the unripe tomatoes in light and sun, and this has worked for me for many times.

21. A way to ripen tomatoes

Key tips

1. Enjoy all the fun of picking and eating your own tomatoes

2. When the season is over bring indoors on the vines to ripen

CHAPTER 7 TROUBLE SHOOTING

Blight

Unfortunately, tomatoes are not without their problems. The best known is probably Blight, a devastating fungus which is air born and prevalent in warm wet summers. It can travel on the wind for distances up to 30 miles which enables it to spread easily, and it tends to make an appearance late in the growing season. Blight starts with brownish patches on the leaves and can very quickly kill a plant, see image 22. The only recommended way to prevent Blight was said to spray with a Bordeaux mixture. This is a mixture of copper, sulphate and lime used as a fungicide, but which was withdrawn in 2013 under EEC regulations. There are some new sprays on the market, the efficacy of which is uncertain. Critically, there is no non chemical treatment which is a problem if you want to grow organically. Truth is I have never sprayed tomato plants with Bordeaux mixture because firstly, Blight is so very difficult to stop once the plants are infected, and secondly I do not want to spray chemicals on my home grown veg.

If Blight is a problem in your area you can grow the more Blight resistant tomatoes or grow in a greenhouse. Fortunately, tomatoes grown in a greenhouse seems to be more protected and in the same growing season, I have had potato Blight in the veg plot but no tomato Blight in the greenhouse. Unfortunately, warm humid and wet conditions are ideal for Blight and these are common in an English Summer. Best tips are (1) take care not to water the leaves of plants, (2) keep bush tomatoes off the ground, and (3) Remove leaves as described above to aid air circulation and (4) if you can, grow some tomatoes in a greenhouse.

If you are growing tomatoes outside where Blight may raise its ugly head, you can try varieties such as 'Fantasio'F1 a Cordon type, 'Latah'F1 a bush with large cherry tomatoes, 'Legend' a beefsteak with RHS AGM. These varieties are said to be Blight resistant but not immune, I cannot vouch for their flavour as I tend to grow varieties of my choice but in a greenhouse.

22. Late Blight on tomatoes

Blight is the worst problem you can get with tomatoes as it strikes so suddenly and is very hard to prevent. By the time you spot it, it tends to be too late.

Fortunately it is not a regular visitor and greenhouse tomatoes seem to give it a miss. At the first signs of Blight remove the plant so it cannot infect others, dispose of it and do not compost it, because the Blight will remain in the soil and can be transferred when you use the compost.

Other problems and diseases

23. Split skins on tomatoes

Split skins on tomatoes is usually caused by irregular watering, which is one of the reasons why it is important to water regularly and ensure the compost is fully moist but not saturated.

Blossom end rot, which is when the underside of the tomato gets a black dark mark which, as the tomato grows, appears as a sunken patch creating a flattened appearance to the tomato. It is caused by lack of calcium, which is caused by lack of water to bring the calcium to the roots. To avoid this problem regular and sufficient watering is vital.

Botrytis, also known as grey mould, can affect tomatoes, and it causes grey fluffy patches on the leaves and mouldy flowers. This is more common in greenhouses and poly tunnels where there are humid conditions and is aggravated by poor ventilation. The best weapon against Botrytis is good ventilation which is key to prevention. At all times over the summer open up vents and doors as often as possible. The lets the bees and air in.

Leaf curl is quite common, and doesn't affect the fruit quality. It is caused by low night temperatures and can be a problem especially at the start of the growing season when it is cooler. As long as the rest of the plant looks healthy leaf curl does not do any permanent damage.

Tomato virus causes brown patterns on the leaves, stunted growth and unsightly marks on the fruit. There are no chemical controls and infected plants need to be removed to reduce the spread and disposed of, not composted. There may be a lot of listed problems and diseases, but in many growing seasons tomatoes can be disease free.

CHAPTER 8 CONCLUSION AND CHECKLIST

Growing Tomatoes Checklist

A summer checklist for growing tomatoes. Note that all dates are approximate depending on the growing conditions and the quality of the spring, summer and autumn.

1. Germinate seedlings in February/March.
2. Pot on into single pots late March.
3. Pot on 4/5 weeks later in late April.
4. Pot on again in late May/June into a final container.
5. Remove side shoots on Cordon tomatoes throughout season.
6. Late May buy mature plants for planting out, harden off first.
7. If growing tomatoes, outside harden off plants in May ready for planting out.
8. When the first flowers appear around May/June onwards start feeding, lightly at first.
9. Ensure plants are regularly watered and fed throughout season.
10. Make holiday watering arrangements for plants.
11. Remove leaves to thin out foliage and aid air circulation from around July onwards
12. July and August enjoy the harvest.
13. Late August or early September take stock remove immature fruits and flowers.
14. In September/October take stock again, and stop plants growing.
15. Harvest more and make soups and sauces with any glut for the freezer.
16. October/November bring in remaining tomatoes to ripen.

And Finally, If All Else Fails.

There are lots of additional and different ways to grow tomatoes, for example, ring culture, upside down, straw bales, gadgets and aids to increase the crop, but I like to keep it simple. By following the method set out in this short guide you will have, as I have had, a tasty crop of sweet tomatoes every year. The essential points are to pot on tomatoes so they are gradually moved up to a large pot; harden off before placing outside; remove all side shoots and some leaves. Stop the plant growing when it has 4/5 trusses or is large enough for your greenhouse and space.

And if you run out of time and do none of these, the absolute essentials are to water and feed regularly and to enjoy growing your own tomatoes.

CHAPTER 9 TABLE OF ILLUSTRATIONS

Printed in Great Britain
by Amazon

42678532R00035